D1532047

ONE-POT
MEALS

JJ VIRGIN

ONE-POT MEALS

RECIPE **INDEX**

WELCOME!

As a busy mom of two boys and the owner of two businesses, I know what it's like to have your hands full! And when it's a late night after a long day, the siren call of the drive-thru can be pretty hard to resist...

Thank goodness for one-pot meals! They're convenient, nutritious, and great in any weather. (I'd much rather use the crockpot in the summertime than heat up the whole kitchen...)

This cookbook features plenty of flavor options, all with only one pot to clean at the end. You don't have to worry about that last minute scramble to figure out what's for dinner because now you've got dozens of meal recipes that are delicious, wholesome, and quick to put together.

Not only do they taste fantastic, the recipes in this cookbook are also great for you! They're approved* for both *The Virgin Diet* and the *Sugar Impact Diet*. That means they're free of inflammatory foods like gluten, soy, dairy, eggs, peanuts, corn, and sweeteners, so your body doesn't suffer when mealtime ends. Not a promise fast food can ever make...

Whether you're watching your waistline, hoping for more energy, or just want to take good care of yourself and your loved ones, now you've got plenty of recipes to do it right.

Best,

JJ

P.S. – If you'd like even more simple healthy recipes, check out **JJVirgin.com/blog** today. We'd love to have you in our community!

Except as noted in certain cycles.

JJ'S EASY STOVETOP LEFTOVERS "STOUP"

MAKES 4 SERVINGS

INGREDIENTS:

- 2 tablespoons olive oil
- 1 cup chopped yellow onion
- 1 cup chopped red bell pepper
- ¼ lb crimini mushrooms, sliced
- 3 stalks celery, chopped
- 2 medium zucchini, halved lengthwise and sliced ½" thick
- 1 crookneck squash, chopped
- 1 tablespoon chopped garlic
- 1 teaspoon dried basil
- 6 cups organic, low-sodium chicken broth
- 1 lb. cooked chicken breast (any leftover chicken will do!)
- 2 cups cooked wild rice (leftover rice or quinoa can be used here)
- Sea salt and pepper to taste

DIRECTIONS:

Melt olive oil in a large saucepan over medium heat.

Add onions, peppers, mushrooms, celery, zucchini and crookneck.

Cook for 5 minutes until vegetables begin to soften and brown, stirring occasionally.

Add garlic and basil and cook an additional 1-2 minutes.

Add broth, bring to a boil, reduce heat, cover and simmer 15 minutes.

Add cooked chicken and wild rice and cook an additional 5 minutes until chicken is warmed through.

Season to taste with salt and pepper.

JJ'S EASY SLOW COOKER "STOUP"

MAKES 4 SERVINGS

INGREDIENTS:

- 1 medium yellow onion, chopped
- ½ lb crimini mushrooms, halved
- 3 carrots, peeled and chopped
- 3 stalks celery, chopped
- 2 medium zucchini, chopped
- 2 crookneck squash, chopped
- 1 tablespoon chopped garlic
- 1 cup uncooked wild rice
- ½ teaspoon dried basil
- 2 boneless, skinless chicken breasts, about 1 lb. total
- 6 cups organic, low-sodium chicken broth
- 1 bunch spinach, chopped
- Sea salt and pepper to taste

DIRECTIONS:

Place onions, mushrooms, carrots, celery, zucchini, crook-neck, garlic, rice, and basil in slow cooker.

Top with chicken breasts and pour broth over mixture.

Place lid on slow cooker and cook for 6 hours on low or about 3½ hours on high.

When chicken is fully cooked and rice is tender, remove chicken and shred using 2 forks. Return chicken to pot, add spinach, and stir to combine. Cook a few minutes until spinach is wilted.

Season to taste with salt and pepper.

MEXICAN LETTUCE WRAP "TACOS"

MAKES 4 SERVINGS

INGREDIENTS:

- 1 teaspoon olive oil
- ¾ lb. grass-fed ground beef
- 1 cup chopped onion
- 1 poblano pepper, seeded and chopped
- 1 jalapeño pepper, seeded and diced
- 2 teaspoons ground cumin
- 2 teaspoons ground coriander
- 1 teaspoon chili powder
- ½ cup vegetable broth
- 1 can black beans, drained and rinsed
- 4 Roma tomatoes, chopped
- 1 (2.25 oz.) can sliced olives
- Salt and pepper to taste
- 1 head romaine lettuce, separated into individual leaves
- 1 avocado, peeled and chopped
- 2 scallions, thinly sliced
- ¼ cup pepitas (pumpkin seeds)

DIRECTIONS:

Heat oil in large skillet over medium high heat.

Add ground beef and cook, breaking it up with the side of a wooden spoon until most of the pink is gone.

Reduce heat to medium. Add onion, peppers, cumin, coriander and chili powder (adding a little more olive oil if not enough fat was rendered and pan is dry), and continue cooking until vegetables are soft and beef is cooked through and no longer pink.

Add vegetable broth, black beans and tomatoes. Continue cooking, stirring occasionally until most of the liquid is absorbed, about 3-5 minutes.

Remove from heat and stir in olives, salt and pepper (about ¼ teaspoon each).

Place two romaine leaves on each of four plates, and press down on the stem to flatten (or remove stem completely and make two smaller wraps out of each leaf).

Using a slotted spoon, divide filling between lettuce leaves, top with avocado, scallions and pepitas. Roll romaine leaves like a taco.

Dijon-Herb Chicken and Vegetables

MAKES 4 SERVINGS

INGREDIENTS:

- 3 tablespoons Dijon mustard
- 3 tablespoons olive oil, divided
- 2 tablespoons coconut aminos
- 1 teaspoon dried basil
- 1 teaspoon dried oergano
- ¼ teaspoon sea salt
- ¼ teaspoon pepper
- 4 bone-in, skin-on chicken organic breasts
- 1 bunch baby rainbow carrots, cut in thirds on the diagonal
- 1 fennel bulb, trimmed and cut into 6 wedges
- 1 red onion, peeled and cut into 6 wedges
- ½ lb. crimini mushrooms
- Sea salt and pepper to taste

DIRECTIONS:

Preheat oven to 400°.

In a small bowl mix together the mustard, 1 tablespoon of the olive oil, coconut aminos, basil, oregano, salt and pepper.

Pat chicken dry with paper towel, place in a bowl and pour marinade over chicken, tossing to coat.

In a large baking dish toss the vegetables with remaining 2 tablespoons olive oil and a pinch of sea salt and pepper.

Nestle the chicken in the vegetables and roast 35-45 minutes until chicken is cooked through to 165° and vegetables are tender.

Thai Noodle Bowl

MAKES 4 SERVINGS

INGREDIENTS:

- 1 tablespoon coconut oil
- 2 baby bok choy, white and green part separated, and chopped
- 1 cup thinly sliced onion
- 4 oz. shiitakes, thinly sliced
- 1 carrot, cut into thin matchsticks
- 1 inch piece of ginger, peeled and minced
- 1 teaspoon chopped garlic
- 2 teaspoons curry powder
- 4 cups vegetable or chicken broth
- 1 stalk lemongrass, pounded and cut into 1" pieces
- 3 cups shredded cooked chicken
- ½ cup unsweetened coconut milk
- 1 package Shirataki noodles, drained and rinsed
- ¼ teaspoon sea salt

DIRECTIONS:

Melt coconut oil in large saucepan over medium heat. Add white part of bok choy, onion, shiitakes and carrot and cook, stirring occasionally until beginning to soften, about 3-4 minutes.

Add ginger, garlic and curry; and cook an additional 1-2 minutes, stirring often. Add broth and lemongrass, increase heat and bring to a gentle boil. Then reduce heat to low, cover and simmer 20 minutes.

Add green parts of bok choy, cooked chicken, coconut milk, shirataki noodles and salt. Continue cooking a few minutes until chicken is warmed through.

NOTE: Lemongrass in this form is for flavor and is not edible; you can remove the pieces (this is why you want to cut them large enough to see) or let your guests know to avoid eating these pieces.

Bean and Bacon Minestrone Soup

MAKES 4 SERVINGS (ABOUT 2 CUPS PER SERVING)

INGREDIENTS:

- 5 slices uncured nitrate-free bacon
- 1 medium red onion, chopped
- 3 celery ribs, chopped
- 6 garlic cloves, chopped
- 1 teaspoon chopped thyme
- ½ teaspoon dried oregano
- 1 medium zucchini, about 12 ounces, cut into ½-inch dice
- 1 (14.5-oz) can organic no-salt-added diced tomatoes
- 3 cups organic low-sodium chicken broth
- 3 cups chopped kale
- 1 (15-oz) can organic no-salt-added cannellini beans, drained and rinsed
- ¾ teaspoon sea salt
- ¼ teaspoon ground black pepper

DIRECTIONS:

Heat a Dutch oven over medium heat. Add the bacon and cook until crisp, turning once, 6–7 minutes. Transfer to a plate covered with paper towel and drain; crumble.

Pour off all but 2 tablespoons bacon fat from the Dutch oven. Return to the stove over medium-high heat. Add the onion, celery, garlic, thyme, and oregano; cook, stirring occasionally, until slightly softened, 4–5 minutes.

Add the zucchini and cook until slightly softened, about 5 minutes. Stir in the diced tomatoes and cook 2 minutes.

Add the broth, bring to a boil, then stir in the kale. Reduce heat to medium and simmer, uncovered, 25 minutes.

Add the beans, quinoa noodles, salt, and pepper and cook until heated through, 2–3 minutes. Divide among four bowls and top with the reserved bacon.

JJ Virgin's Sugar Impact Diet, Grand Central 2014

Texas Bison Chili

MAKES 4 SERVINGS (ABOUT 1¼ CUPS PER SERVING)

INGREDIENTS:

- 1 tablespoon palm fruit oil, sustainably farmed
- 1 pound grass-fed ground bison
- 2 medium onions, chopped
- 3 garlic cloves, minced
- 1 medium green bell pepper, chopped
- 2 tablespoons chili powder
- 1 teaspoon dried oregano
- 1 teaspoon ground cumin
- ¼ teaspoon ground chipotle pepper
- 2 (14.5-oz.) cans organic no-salt-added fire-roasted diced tomatoes
- 1 (15-oz.) can organic no-salt-added red kidney beans, drained and rinsed
- ¾ teaspoon sea salt
- ¼ teaspoon ground black pepper

DIRECTIONS:

Heat the oil in a Dutch oven over medium-high heat. Add the bison and cook, breaking into smaller clumps with a spoon, until no longer pink, about 4–5 minutes. Stir in the onions, garlic, bell pepper, chili powder, oregano, cumin, and ground chipotle; cook, stirring occasionally, until the vegetables are slightly softened, 3–4 minutes.

Add the diced tomatoes; bring to a boil; reduce heat to medium-low cover, and simmer, stirring occasionally, 30 minutes.

Stir in the beans, return to a simmer and cook 5 minutes. Remove from the heat and stir in the salt and pepper.

JJ Virgin's Sugar Impact Diet, Grand Central 2014

Barker Brunswick Stew

MAKES 4 SERVINGS

INGREDIENTS:

- ½ lb ground elk or bison
- ½ lb ground turkey
- 6 scallions, chopped
- 1 tablespoon olive oil
- 1 large green bell pepper, chopped
- 4 cups whole canned tomatoes, undrained
- 1 (15-oz) can great Northern beans, undrained
- 2 cups matchstick-cut turnips
- 2 cups bite-sized cauliflower florets
- 1 cup okra, sliced (if frozen, thaw and drain first)
- 1 tablespoon ground flax seed
- Sea salt and pepper to taste

DIRECTIONS:

In a large skillet over medium heat brown meat until no longer pink. Remove from skillet and keep warm.

In same skillet, heat olive oil and sauté onions and bell pepper until softened, about 5 minutes. Add tomatoes and beans (and their liquid), turnips, cauliflower, okra, flax seed, salt and pepper. Bring to a boil, reduce heat, return meat to skillet and simmer 45-60 minutes.

The Virgin Diet Community Cookbook, Contributed by Regina Barker

One-Skillet Bacon Burger Hash

MAKES 2 SERVINGS

INGREDIENTS:

- 4 slices organic, nitrate-free bacon
- 1 medium sweet potato
- 1 medium onion
- 1 red bell pepper
- ½ lb grass-fed ground beef
- ½ teaspoon onion powder
- ½ teaspoon garlic powder
- ½ teaspoon chili powder
- 4 cups baby spinach
- Sea salt and pepper to taste

DIRECTIONS:

Remove meats from refrigerator and let sit at room temperature for 10 minutes. Cook bacon in skillet to desired doneness, remove from skillet, and set aside. Reserve 2-3 tablespoons bacon fat; drain the rest.

While bacon is cooking process the sweet potato, onion and bell pepper using the shredding blade of your food processor. Once shredded, place vegetables in cheesecloth and twist to remove excess moisture.

Add 2 tablespoons reserved bacon fat to same skillet over medium heat and add sweet potato, onion and bell pepper. Season with salt and pepper and cook, stirring occasionally until crispy and browned, about 5-8 minutes.

Meanwhile mix beef, onion powder, garlic powder and chili powder in a medium bowl. Form into 2 patties.

Remove hash to a plate and keep warm.

Add patties to skillet and cook, turning once, until cooked through, about 8-10 minutes. Remove patties to plate and keep warm.

Add remaining reserved fat (1 teaspoon- 1 tablespoon as needed) to skillet and add spinach, salt and pepper to taste. Cook until spinach is wilted.

To assemble, divide sweet potato mixture between 2 plates. Top with spinach and 2 pieces of crumbled bacon. Place beef burger on top.

The Virgin Diet Community Cookbook, contributed by Lindsey Neely

Yes or no to gluten? Paleo or vegan?
Which supplements do you really need?

Trade the guesswork for helpful,
science-based health and nutrition news
you can trust at JJVirgin.com/blog.

Caribbean Chicken Stew

MAKES 8 SERVINGS

INGREDIENTS:

- 1½ tablespoons olive oil
- 1 large yellow onion, chopped
- 1 red, orange or yellow bell pepper, diced
- 3-4 large garlic cloves, crushed
- 1 bay leaf
- 2 teaspoons cinnamon
- 1 teaspoon allspice,
- 1 teaspoon nutmeg
- ½ teaspoon cayenne
- 1 (16-oz.) can no-sugar-added diced tomatoes
- 2 cups low-sodium chicken broth
- 1 (15-oz.) can black beans, undrained
- 1½ lbs. poached skinless, boneless chicken breasts, shredded
- 1½ cups thick-sliced zucchini half-moons
- Sea salt and freshly ground pepper

DIRECTIONS:

Heat oil in a large pot over medium heat.

Add onion, bell peppers and garlic and sauté 3 minutes. Add bay leaf, cinnamon, allspice, nutmeg and cayenne and continue cooling 3 minutes. Add tomatoes, stock, and beans. Simmer covered for 15 minutes, stirring occasionally.

Add chicken and zucchini and simmer, covered for an additional 10 minutes. Remove bay leaf. Season to taste with salt and pepper.

The Virgin Diet Community Cookbook, contributed by Judy LaBelle

Chicken Chili

MAKES 4-6 SERVINGS

INGREDIENTS:

- 1 teaspoon each: paprika, cumin, chopped cilantro
- Sea salt and pepper to taste
- 1 lb. skinless boneless chicken breast
- 2 tablespoons coconut or olive oil, divided
- 1 red or yellow pepper, chopped
- 1 sweet onion, chopped
- 8 oz mushrooms, sliced
- 2 garlic cloves, chopped
- 2-3 Roma tomatoes, chopped
- 6 oz. low-sodium vegetable juice
- 1 (15-oz.) can black beans
- 1 tablespoon cumin
- 1 teaspoon chili powder
- Fresh cilantro sprigs to garnish

DIRECTIONS:

In a small bowl, mix paprika, cumin, cilantro, salt and pepper. Rub mixture onto chicken breast.

Heat the oil and cook chicken until browned and cooked through. Remove from skillet and keep warm.

Heat additional tablespoon of oil in skillet and sauté the bell pepper, onion, mushrooms, and the garlic until soft

Chop the chicken into bite-sized pieces and add to the cooked vegetables. Add the Roma tomatoes, tomato juice and beans. Add the cumin and chili powder according to your taste. Cover and simmer 20 minutes.

Pour into bowls and garnish with chopped cilantro.

The Virgin Diet Community Cookbook, contributed by Genise Carter

Susan's Chili

MAKES 8-10 SERVINGS

INGREDIENTS:

- 1 tablespoon olive oil
- 1 lb. ground grass-fed beef
- 2-3 tablespoons chili powder
- ½-1 teaspoon cumin
- ½-1 teaspoon chipotle chile powder
- ½-1 teaspoon cayenne pepper
- ½-1 teaspoon black pepper
- 1 (28-oz.) can crushed tomatoes
- 1 (28-oz.) can tomato puree
- 1 (14-oz.) can diced tomatoes with jalapeños
- 1 (14-oz.) can diced tomatoes
- 1 medium onion, diced
- 1-2 bell peppers, diced
- 1-2 jalapeños, seeded and diced
- 4 (14-oz.) cans beans, rinsed and drained, (black, kidney, pinto)
- 1 avocado, chopped
- Cilantro for garnish

DIRECTIONS:

Heat olive oil in a large saucepan over medium heat and sauté ground beef until no longer pink. Stir in chili powder, cumin, chipotle chile powder, cayenne and black pepper and cook for a minute or so.

Add tomatoes, onions, bell pepper, jalapeño and beans and simmer over medium low heat for 2-3 hours.

Serve topped with avocado and cilantro.

The Virgin Diet Community Cookbook, contributed by Susan Helmuth

Turkey, Beans and Greens

MAKES 2 SERVINGS

INGREDIENTS:

- **1 tablespoon coconut oil**
- **1 onion, chopped**
- **2 teaspoons minced garlic**
- **1 lb. ground turkey**
- **1 (16-oz.) can black, adzuki or great Northern beans**
- **2-3 cups kale, bok choy, and/or beet greens**
- **Sea salt and pepper to taste**

DIRECTIONS:

Heat coconut oil in a large skillet and sauté onion until translucent, about 3-5 minutes. Add garlic and stir for a few minutes.

Add turkey and stir and break up into pieces with a wooden spoon. Brown turkey until no longer pink. Add beans and veggies. Cook until greens are wilted.

Season to taste with salt and pepper.

The Virgin Diet Community Cookbook, contributed by Kimberly Fox

Asian Stir Fry

MAKES 4 SERVINGS

INGREDIENTS:

- 1 tablespoon red palm oil
- 1 tablespoon sesame oil
- 1 onion, chopped
- 1 cup red bell pepper, chopped
- 1 cup zucchini, chopped
- 1 cup mushrooms, chopped
- 2 cloves garlic, minced
- 1 cup cooked chicken, cut into bite-sized pieces
- 1 cup cooked shrimp, cut into bite-sized pieces
- 1 cup organic chicken broth
- 2 tablespoons coconut aminos
- 1 teaspoon rice wine vinegar
- 2 teaspoons freshly grated ginger
- 1 teaspoon cumin
- Pinch red pepper flakes
- Sea salt and pepper to taste
- 1 tablespoon brown rice flour dissolved in ¼ cup COLD water
- 1 cup rice noodles rehydrated in HOT water for 8 minutes then drained

DIRECTIONS:

Heat the oils in large skillet or wok over medium-high heat.

Add onion, bell pepper, zucchini, mushrooms and garlic and stir fry until they are crisp-tender.

Add the chicken and shrimp and toss until heated through.

Add broth, coconut aminos, rice vinegar, ginger, cumin and red pepper flakes and bring all to a boil.

Add the dissolved flour to thicken the sauce, stirring frequently until sauce is thickened.

Add the noodles, tossing to coat. Heat through, approximately 2-3 minutes.

Serve with some coconut aminos on the side if desired.

The Virgin Diet Community Cookbook, contributed by Coleen Wheeler

If you love healthy, delicious recipes that are ready in minutes, you can get plenty free at JJVirgin.com/recipes now!

Tarragon Soup

MAKES 4-6 SERVINGS

INGREDIENTS:

- 1 lb. grass-fed ground beef or 1 lb free-range ground chicken
- 2½- 3 cups chopped onions
- 7-8 celery stalks, chopped
- 2 small cloves garlic, crushed
- 2 quarts organic chicken broth or vegetable broth
- 3 cups water
- 3 (15-oz.) cans great Northern beans, rinsed and drained
- 2 (14.5-oz.) cans organic chopped tomatoes
- 2 tablespoons fresh tarragon
- 2 tablespoons fresh basil
- 1½ teaspoons fresh oregano
- Salt and pepper to taste

DIRECTIONS:

Brown ground beef in a large soup pot, smashing it with a wooden spoon so that you don't have any large chunks of meat.

Add onion, celery and garlic. Stir and cook for 3 to 5 minutes.

Add broth and water. Bring to a boil, reduce heat to medium and cook for 1 hour.

Add beans, tomatoes, tarragon, basil and oregano. Stir to combine, reduce heat and simmer for at least another hour, stirring occasionally.

Season to taste with salt and pepper.

The Virgin Diet Community Cookbook, contributed by Cynthia Knight

White Chili

MAKES 4 SERVINGS

INGREDIENTS:

- 1 tablespoon olive oil
- 1 lb. boneless chicken breast, cut in ½" cubes
- 1 medium onion, chopped
- 1½ teaspoons garlic powder
- 2 (15-oz.) cans great Northern beans, rinsed and drained
- 1 (14.5-oz.) can chicken broth
- 2 (4-oz.) cans chopped green chiles
- 1 teaspoon sea salt
- 1 teaspoon cumin
- 1 teaspoon dried oregano
- 1 teaspoon cayenne pepper
- ½ teaspoon black pepper

DIRECTIONS:

Heat oil in large skillet over medium heat. Sauté chicken, onion, and garlic powder until chicken is no longer pink.

Add beans, broth, chiles and seasonings. Bring to a boil, reduce heat and simmer uncovered for 30 minutes.

Remove from heat and serve.

The Virgin Diet Community Cookbook, contributed by Karen Weightman

Mary's Veggie Quesadilla Sauté

MAKES 6 SERVINGS

INGREDIENTS:

- 1 tablespoons olive oil
- ½ red onion, chopped
- 3 cloves garlic, crushed
- 8 mini bell peppers (red, orange, yellow), chopped
- 6 cups fresh baby spinach
- 1 (4-oz.) can diced green chiles
- 1 (15-oz.) can black beans, rinsed and drained
- 1 (15-oz.) can kidney beans, rinsed and drained
- 1 tablespoon chili powder
- ¼ teaspoon red pepper flakes (or ½ serrano pepper chopped)
- 1 teaspoon sea salt
- ½ teaspoon black pepper
- 3 brown rice tortillas, torn in 2" pieces
- 1 avocado, sliced
- 1 jalapeño pepper, seeded and chopped
- 1 cup shredded cabbage
- ½ cup sliced black olives

DIRECTIONS:

Heat oil in large skillet over medium heat. Add onions, garlic, and peppers, and sauté for a few minutes. Add spinach and green chiles and continue cooking about 5 minutes. Add beans, chili powder, red pepper flakes, salt, pepper and tortillas pieces. Sauté until veggies and tortillas are cooked. Remove from heat.

Top with avocado, jalapeño pepper, cabbage and olives.

The Virgin Diet Community Cookbook, contributed by Mary Snyder

Peter Pumpkin Eater's Turkey Chili

MAKES 4 SERVINGS

INGREDIENTS:

- **1 tablespoon olive oil**
- **1½ pounds lean ground turkey**
- **1 medium red onion, chopped**
- **3 cloves garlic, pressed**
- **1 medium red bell pepper, de-seeded, de-ribbed and chopped**
- **1 (16-oz.) can pumpkin puree**
- **1 (28-oz.) can diced tomatoes**
- **3 tablespoons cider vinegar**
- **1 tablespoon tomato paste**
- **1 tablespoon raw honey**
- **1 teaspoon ground cumin**
- **1 teaspoon cayenne pepper**
- **½ teaspoon paprika**
- **½ teaspoon ground cinnamon**

DIRECTIONS:

Heat the oil in a large skillet over medium-high heat. Add turkey; cook and crumble till no longer pink then transfer to a large slow cooker. Add remaining ingredients and give mixture a good stir.*

Cover and cook on HIGH for 2 or 3 hours.

*LEANNE'S NOTE: If you think your chili is too thick, just add a splash of water.

The Virgin Diet Holiday Guide, contributed by Leanne Ely

Red Lentil Stew

MAKES 6 SERVINGS

INGREDIENTS:

- 2 tablespoons extra virgin olive oil
- ½ onion, diced
- 2 tablespoons garlic, minced
- 2 teaspoons black mustard seeds
- 1 teaspoon cumin
- 1 teaspoon turmeric
- ½ teaspoon coriander
- 1 small carrot, diced
- 2 cups cauliflower, small florets
- 1¼ cups red lentils, rinsed
- 6 cups water
- 1 cup tomato, diced
- 2 cups broccoli, small florets
- ½ teaspoon sea salt
- 1 tablespoon lemon juice
- Chopped fresh parsley or cilantro for garnish

DIRECTIONS:

Heat olive oil in a large soup pot on medium heat.

Sauté onions and garlic until tender. Add mustard seeds and stir until they begin to pop. Add other spices and sauté one minute. Add carrot and cauliflower and stir to coat.

Add lentils and water and bring to a boil.

Reduce to low and simmer until lentils are soft, about 25 minutes. Add tomato, broccoli, and salt and continue to simmer 5 more minutes.

Just before serving, stir in lemon juice and sprinkle with parsley or cilantro.

The Virgin Diet Companion Cookbook, contributed by Dr. Mark Hyman, www.drhyman.com

Roasted Roots with Turkey

MAKES 4 SERVINGS

INGREDIENTS:

- 1 small carrot, diced
- 1 small yam, peeled and diced
- 1 small onion, diced
- 1 small beet, peeled and diced
- ½ red pepper, remove seeds then dice
- ½ pound organic ground turkey
- 1 tablespoon extra virgin olive oil
- 1 teaspoon dried sage
- ½ teaspoon dried basil
- ¼ teaspoon sea salt
- Pinch black pepper
- ¼ teaspoon chili pepper (optional)

DIRECTIONS:

Pre-heat oven to 375 degrees.

In a large bowl, mix all ingredients until well combined.

Place in a baking dish and cover.

Bake for 20 minutes, then bake uncovered for another 10 minutes to crisp vegetables.

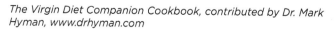

The Virgin Diet Companion Cookbook, contributed by Dr. Mark Hyman, www.drhyman.com

Mexican Chicken Tortilla Soup

MAKES 4 SERVINGS

INGREDIENTS:

- 4 teaspoons olive oil or coconut oil, divided
- 1 brown rice tortilla, cut in half then in thin strips
- 1 medium onion, chopped
- 2 garlic cloves, minced
- 2 celery stalks, chopped
- 1 teaspoon ground cumin
- 1 teaspoon dried basil
- ¼ teaspoon ground chipotle pepper
- 1 (15-oz.) can black beans, rinsed and drained
- 1 (14.5-oz.) can organic fire roasted diced tomatoes
- 4 cups organic low sodium chicken broth
- 12 ounces cooked organic free range boneless skinless chicken breast, cut into cubes, 2 cups
- 2 tablespoons chopped fresh cilantro
- 1 tablespoon lime juice
- ½ teaspoon sea salt
- 1 avocado, cut into ½-inch dice

DIRECTIONS:

Heat 3 teaspoons of the oil in a Dutch oven over medium high. Add tortilla strips and cook, stirring, until crisp, about 5-6 minutes. Transfer to a plate lined with a paper towel and drain.

Return Dutch oven to the stove and heat the remaining 1 teaspoon oil. Add the onion, garlic, celery, cumin, basil and ground chipotle. Cook, stirring occasionally, until the vegetables begin to soften, 2-3 minutes.

Stir in the tomatoes and cook 2 minutes. Pour in the broth, bring to a boil and immediately reduce heat to medium low, cover and simmer 25 minutes.

Stir in the chicken and black beans and cook until heated through, 3 minutes. Remove from the heat and stir in the cilantro, lime juice and salt.

Divide the soup among four bowls and top with the tortilla strips and avocado.

Adapted from The Virgin Diet Cookbook, Grand Central 2014

For more fun, nutritious recipes
and easy tips to help you lose weight and
take great care of yourself and your family,
check out JJVirgin.com/blog today.

Mushroom Beef Stew

MAKES 4 SERVINGS

INGREDIENTS:

- 1 pound grass fed beef round roast, cut into 1-inch cubes
- ¾ teaspoon sea salt, divided
- ½ teaspoon freshly ground black pepper, divided
- 2 tablespoons arrowroot
- 2 tablespoons macadamia nut oil
- 1 large onion, coarsely chopped, about 1½ cups
- 8 ounces white mushrooms, sliced
- 4 ounces shiitake mushrooms, stemmed and sliced
- 1 tablespoon fresh thyme leaves
- 4 garlic cloves, minced
- 3 celery stalks, cut into 1-inch pieces
- 2/3 cup dry red wine
- 3 tablespoons tomato paste
- 2 cups organic low sodium beef broth
- 1 small sweet potato, 6 ounces, peeled and cut into 3/4-inch cubes

DIRECTIONS:

Season the beef, ¼ teaspoon of the salt and ¼ teaspoon of the pepper in a medium bowl. Add the arrowroot and toss well to coat.

Heat 1 tablespoon of the oil in a Dutch oven over medium-high. Add the beef and cook, turning occasionally, until browned, about 4-5 minutes. Transfer to a plate.

Return the Dutch oven to stove and heat the remaining 1 tablespoon oil over medium.

Add the onion, mushrooms and thyme and cook, stirring occasionally, until slightly browned, about 8-9 minutes.

Stir in the garlic and celery and cook 2 minutes. Stir in the wine and tomato paste and bring to a boil and cook 1 minute. Add the broth and reserved beef, return to a boil, immediately reduce heat to medium-low, cover and gently simmer 40 minutes until beef is nearly tender.

Stir in the sweet potato, return to a gentle simmer, and cook until beef and potato are tender, about 20 minutes longer.

JJ Virgin's first *NYT* bestseller was *The Virgin Diet*, a ground-breaking elimination diet that can help you discover your food intolerances. Food intolerances have been linked to weight gain, autoimmune disease, leaky gut, and more. Learn more at JJVirgin.com/Programs

Turkey Chili

MAKES 4 SERVINGS

INGREDIENTS:

- 1 tablespoon palm fruit oil
- 1 medium onion, chopped
- 4 garlic cloves, minced
- 1 large green bell pepper, chopped
- 1 pound natural lean ground turkey
- 5 teaspoons chili powder
- 1 teaspoon smoked paprika
- ½ teaspoon dried oregano
- 2 (14.5-oz.) cans fire-roasted diced tomatoes
- 2 tablespoons tomato paste
- 1 (15-oz.) can organic no-salt-added red kidney beans, drained and rinsed
- ½ teaspoon sea salt
- ¼ teaspoon freshly ground black pepper

DIRECTIONS:

Heat the oil in a Dutch oven over medium-high heat. Add the onion, garlic and bell pepper and cook, stirring occasionally, until the vegetables begin to soften, 2-3 minutes.

Add the turkey and cook, breaking it into smaller pieces with a wooden spoon until no longer pink, about 5-6 minutes. Stir in the chili powder, paprika and oregano and cook 1 minute. Add the tomatoes and tomato paste, bring to a boil and immediately reduce the heat to medium-low; cover and simmer, stirring occasionally, 30 minutes or until slightly thickened.

Stir in the beans and cook 5 minutes longer. Remove from the heat and stir in the salt and pepper.

For spicy chili, replace 1 teaspoon of the chili powder with 1 teaspoon hot Mexican chile powder.

The Virgin Diet Cookbook, Grand Central 2014

Lentil, Kale, and Sausage Stew

MAKES 4 SERVINGS

INGREDIENTS:

- 1 tablespoon olive oil
- 1 medium onion, chopped
- 3 garlic, minced
- 3 celery stalks, chopped
- 1 carrot, chopped
- 2 nitrate-free fully cooked organic sweet Italian sausage, halved lengthwise and sliced
- 8 ounces red or green kale, woody stems removed, coarsely chopped
- 1 cup organic sprouted green lentils (such as TruRoots)
- 4 cups organic low sodium chicken broth
- 3 sprigs fresh thyme
- ½ teaspoon sea salt
- ¼ teaspoon freshly ground black pepper

DIRECTIONS:

Heat the oil in a large saucepan over medium-high. Add the onion, garlic, celery and carrot; cook, stirring occasionally, until somewhat softened, 5-6 minutes. Stir in the sausage and cook until vegetables start to brown, about 3 minutes. Add the kale and cook, stirring, until wilted, about 1½-2 minutes.

Add the lentils, broth and thyme; bring to a boil, immediately reduce heat to medium-low, cover and simmer until lentils are tender, about 22-25 minutes. Remove from the heat and season with salt and pepper.

The Virgin Diet Cookbook, Grand Central 2014

Vegetarian Chili

MAKES 4 SERVINGS

INGREDIENTS:

- 4 teaspoons coconut oil or palm fruit oil
- 1 medium onion, chopped
- 4 garlic cloves, minced
- 1 medium green bell pepper, chopped
- 1 medium red bell pepper, chopped
- 2 tablespoons chili powder
- 2 teaspoons ground cumin
- 1 teaspoon dried oregano
- 1 teaspoon ground ancho chili pepper
- 1 (15-oz.) can organic no-salt-added red kidney beans, drained and rinsed
- 1 (15-oz.) can organic no-salt-added black beans, drained and rinsed
- 1 (14.5-oz.) can organic fire-roasted diced tomatoes
- 1 scoop **JJ Virgin's All-In-One Chocolate Shake Powder***, liquefied in 1/3 cup water
- ½ teaspoon sea salt

DIRECTIONS:

Heat the oil in a Dutch oven over medium-high. Add the onion, garlic and bell peppers; cook, stirring occasionally, until slightly softened, 6-7 minutes.

Add the chili powder, cumin, oregano and ancho chili; cook, stirring, 30 seconds. Add the beans, tomatoes and ½ cup water; bring to a boil and reduce heat to medium-low.

Simmer, covered, stirring occasionally, until slightly thickened, 22-24 minutes. Remove from the heat and stir in the protein powder, salt, and pepper.

The Virgin Diet Cookbook, Grand Central 2014

* Available for purchase at **JJVirginStore.com**

Yellow Beet "Borscht" with Lamb

MAKES 6 SERVINGS

INGREDIENTS:

* 2 cups yellow beets peeled, cubed to 2"
* 2 lbs organic lamb stew meat, cubed
* 1 white onion, minced
* 1 tablespoon olive oil
* 3 carrots peeled, sliced ¼ inch
* 3 cloves garlic minced
* 1 bay leaf
* 3 cloves garlic
* 1 head cabbage, sliced ¼ inch
* 2 tablespoon apple cider vinegar
* 1 cup brown rice
* 2 cups organic chicken stock
* 1 cup organic veggie stock

DIRECTIONS:

In a medium pot filled with both stocks, boil the beets about 20 minutes or until fork tender.

In a large pot on medium heat, add the olive oil and then sweat the onions and garlic. Add in the lamb and brown about 5 minutes. Add in the stock with the beets and mix.

Add in the bay leaf, cloves, vinegar and rice. Allow to simmer about 30 minutes or until the rice is soft.

Add in the cabbage until it wilts in about 5 minutes. With a slotted spoon, fish out the cloves and bay leaf. Season with sea salt and fresh cracked pepper to taste.

JJ'S TIP: *You can also make this stew with red beets, but expect a red color and be careful because beets stain. This dish is traditionally served with a dollop of sour cream but you can use a teaspoon of unsweetened cultured coconut milk to give it an extra creaminess.*

White Chicken Chili

MAKES 4 SERVINGS

INGREDIENTS:

- 2 tablespoons olive oil
- 3 cloves garlic, pressed
- 1 cup minced onion
- 1 medium green bell pepper, seeded, deribbed and diced
- 4 (6-oz.) boneless skinless chicken breast halves, cut into 1-inch cubes
- 2 teaspoons chili powder
- 1 tablespoon ground cumin
- 1½ cups diced zucchini
- 1½ cups diced yellow squash
- ¼ cup chopped fresh cilantro
- ½ teaspoon salt
- Freshly ground black pepper, to taste
- 1 (15-oz.) can gluten-free white beans, drained and rinsed
- 2 cups gluten-free chicken broth

DIRECTIONS:

Heat the olive oil in a large saucepan; add garlic, onion and bell pepper and saute until onion is translucent. Add chicken; cook and stir until cooked through.

Add chili powder and stir for 1 minute. Add remaining ingredients and cook until zucchini and yellow squash are tender. Adjust seasonings to taste. Serve hot.

Leanne's Note: Partially frozen chicken is easier to cut.

Break Free Bootcamp, contributed by Leanne Ely

Good Old Beef Stew

MAKES 6 SERVINGS (LEFTOVERS!)

INGREDIENTS:

- 1 pound lean beef stew meat
- 1/3 cup arrowroot flour
- 1½ teaspoons salt
- ½ teaspoon freshly ground black pepper
- 3 tablespoons olive oil
- 6 cups hot water
- 1½ tablespoons gluten-free Worcestershire sauce
- 4 bay leaves
- ½ teaspoon allspice
- 1 large onion, sliced
- 2 carrots, cut up
- 2 sweet potatoes

DIRECTIONS:

Cut beef into 1-inch cubes and remove any fat. Place in a mixing bowl with arrowroot flour, salt and pepper; toss to coat completely.

Heat the oil in a large saucepan or Dutch oven until hot; add beef and brown on all sides and remove to a paper towel-lined plate.

Gradually add the hot water to the saucepan or Dutch oven and scrape up all of the browned bits from the bottom (the flour will have stuck to the pan, but after about 10 minutes it will come loose and blend with the water). Add Worcestershire, bay leaves and allspice to the saucepan or Dutch oven and return browned beef; cover and simmer for 30 minutes.

Add onion, carrots and sweet potatoes; bring to a boil then reduce heat, cover and simmer for about 1 hour or until vegetables are tender.

Remove bay leaves and serve.

Break Free Bootcamp, contributed by Leanne Ely

Ground Beef, Black Bean and Mushroom Skillet

MAKES 4 SERVINGS

INGREDIENTS:

- 1 pound 95% lean ground grass fed beef
- 2/3 teaspoons onion powder
- 1 teaspoon minced garlic
- 6 ounces sliced fresh mushrooms
- 10 ounces canned black beans, rinsed and drained
- 10 ounces low-sodium diced tomatoes
- 1 cup chopped zucchini
- 1 teaspoon dried basil
- 1 teaspoon dried oregano
- ¼ teaspoon sea salt
- ¼ teaspoon freshly ground pepper

DIRECTIONS:

In a skillet, cook the beef, onion and garlic over medium heat until meat is no longer pink; drain juices.

Add mushrooms and sauté until starting to soften. Stir in the black beans, tomatoes, zucchini, basil, oregano, salt and pepper. Cover and simmer for 10 to 15 minutes or until heated through and zucchini is tender.

Break Free Bootcamp, contributed by Leanne Ely

Vegetable Stir Fry

MAKES 4 SERVINGS

INGREDIENTS:

- 2 tablespoons coconut oil
- 1 large onion, thinly sliced
- ½ lb cremini mushrooms, thinly sliced
- 1 large carrot, cut into thin matchsticks
- 1 red or orange bell pepper, cut into thin strips and halved
- 1 head broccoli, cut into small florets
- 1 tablespoon chopped garlic
- ½ cup vegetable broth
- ¼ cup coconut aminos, plus additional for finish
- 1 zucchini, quartered and sliced thinly
- 4 cups shredded purple cabbage (about ½ a small head)
- 1 (15 oz.) can garbanzo beans, drained and rinsed
- ¼ teaspoon sea salt
- Pinch freshly cracked pepper
- Pinch red pepper flakes (optional)
- ¼ cup slivered almonds

DIRECTIONS:

Melt coconut oil in large skillet over medium high heat. Add onion, mushrooms, carrot, bell pepper, and broccoli. Cook 5 minutes, stirring occasionally until lightly softened.

Add garlic (and a little more coconut oil if pan is too dry) and cook an additional minute. Stir in broth and coconut aminos, scraping the bottom of the pan to remove any browned bits.

Add zucchini, cabbage and garbanzo beans stirring to wilt cabbage, cooking a few minutes until crisp tender.

Season with salt, pepper and red pepper flakes, if using. Drizzle with a little more coconut aminos if desired and top with almonds.

Black Bean and Butternut Squash Chili

MAKES 4 SERVINGS

INGREDIENTS:

- **2 tablespoons extra virgin olive oil**
- **1 medium yellow onion, chopped**
- **1 celery stalk, chopped**
- **1 medium carrot, diced**
- **1 tablespoon chopped shallot**
- **1 jalapeño pepper, seeded and chopped**
- **2 teaspoons chopped garlic**
- **2 cups peeled, diced butternut squash**
- **2½ cups vegetable broth**
- **3 (15-oz.) cans black beans, drained and rinsed**
- **2 cups chopped tomato**
- **2 tablespoons chili powder**
- **1 teaspoon cumin**
- **1 teaspoon coriander**
- **1 tablespoon lime juice**
- **Salt & pepper to taste**
- **Pinch cayenne, optional**

DIRECTIONS:

Heat oil in a large saucepan over medium heat.

Add onion, celery, carrot and shallot and sauté. 4-5 minutes until softened. Add jalapeño pepper and garlic and cook 2 minutes, stirring occasionally. Add butternut and sauté for 2 minutes, stirring occasionally.

Stir in the veg broth, beans, tomatoes, chili powder, cumin and coriander. Bring to a boil, reduce heat, and cover and simmer 15-20 minutes until butternut is tender.

Stir in lime juice and season to taste with salt, pepper and cayenne, if using.

Sugar Impact Diet 2-Week Cookbook

Turkey Stew

MAKES 4 SERVINGS

INGREDIENTS:

- 1 tablespoon olive or coconut oil
- 1 yellow onion, diced
- 1 lb. organic ground turkey
- Herbamare, Celtic sea salt, black pepper to taste
- 4 cups vegetables, diced (celery, carrots, butternut squash, Brussels sprouts etc.)
- 1 can cannellini beans, drained
- 2 big handfuls baby kale
- 3 cloves of garlic

DIRECTIONS:

In a soup pot, heat oil on medium heat. Add onions and sauté for a couple of minutes.

Add turkey and cook for about 5-7 minutes, stirring occasionally.

Season with Herbamare, Celtic sea salt, and black pepper. Add vegetables and cover with water.

Bring to a boil, turn to simmer, and cook for 20 minutes.

Add cannellini beans, kale, and garlic. Simmer for 5 more minutes.

Contributed by Sugar Impact Diet Community Member, Petra Mercier

Roast Chicken with Winter Vegetables

MAKES 6 SERVINGS

INGREDIENTS:

- 3½ lbs. organic, free-range chicken, cut up into pieces, or left whole
- 6-8 cups mixed winter vegetables (Mary uses Brussels sprouts, cauliflower, red onion, carrots, and celery)
- 2 small acorn squash, sliced
- 5 slices of nitrate-free bacon, cut into 1 inch pieces
- 2 tablespoons olive oil, divided
- 2 teaspoons sea salt, divided
- 1 teaspoon freshly ground black pepper, divided
- 1 tablespoon fresh rosemary, chopped and divided
- 1 tablespoon fresh thyme, chopped and divided
- ½ teaspoon ground cinnamon

DIRECTIONS:

Preheat oven to 400°F.

Put the mixed vegetables in the bottom of a large roasting pan. Sprinkle the acorn squash slices evenly with cinnamon and add to the roasting pan with the other vegetables.

Season with half of the following ingredients (the other half of these ingredients will be used to season the chicken): olive oil, rosemary, thyme, salt and pepper.

Place bacon pieces evenly over the vegetables.

Top vegetables and squash mixture with the chicken pieces (or whole chicken) Season the chicken with the remaining olive oil, rosemary, thyme, sea salt, and pepper.

Place on the middle rack in the oven. Roast until the chicken registers 170° with an instant-read thermometer, about 60-70 minutes (depending on if using pieces or whole chicken).

Serve chicken with a mixture of the vegetables and acorn squash.

Contributed by Sugar Impact Diet Community Member Mary Cassler

Beef Chili

MAKES 5-6 SERVINGS

INGREDIENTS:

- 1½ lbs lean grass-fed ground beef (can substitute chicken or turkey)
- 1 cup chopped organic walnuts
- 1 large organic yellow onion, chopped
- 2 organic garlic cloves, minced
- 1 organic yellow bell pepper, seeded & chopped
- 1 organic orange bell pepper, seeded & chopped
- 2 Serrano peppers, seeded and minced (can also use jalapeño peppers)
- 1½ cups organic white mushrooms, chopped
- 1 (28 oz.) can organic diced tomatoes, including juice
- 1 (15 oz.) can organic pinto beans, drained
- 1 (15 oz.) can organic black beans, drained
- 2 teaspoons dried oregano
- 1 teaspoon cumin
- 1 teaspoon freshly ground black pepper
- 1 tablespoon chili powder
- 1 teaspoon Himalayan pink sea salt
- 1 teaspoon cayenne (optional)

DIRECTIONS:

Brown beef, with onion, garlic and peppers in a large pot/pan, at least 4 qt, over medium heat, until beef is fully cooked and the veggies are cooked to your liking.

Add the spices, beans, and walnuts. Stir together for 1 minute. Add the mushrooms and tomatoes (with the juice), and bring to a boil.

Lower heat, cover, and simmer on low for 10-15 minutes.

Contributed by Sugar Impact Diet Community Member Carol C.

Stuffed Peppers and Cabbage Soup

MAKES 8-10 SERVINGS (ABOUT ½ CUP PER SERVING

INGREDIENTS:

- 1-2 tablespoons coconut oil
- 1 onion, chopped
- 1 lb. grass-fed ground beef
- ¾ cup uncooked brown rice
- 1 green pepper, cut into ½ inch pieces
- ½ head large green cabbage, thinly julienned
- 1 (32 oz.) organic chicken or beef stock.
- 1 (8 oz.) can organic tomato sauce
- 2 (14.5 oz.) cans organic diced tomatoes
- 2 cups water
- 1 tablespoon dried oregano
- ½ tablespoon dried basil
- 1 teaspoon sea salt
- ½ teaspoon freshly ground black pepper

DIRECTIONS:

Heat a large Dutch oven on the stove over medium-high heat. Add coconut oil. Sauté onion, beef, and rice stirring frequently. Be careful not to let the rice burn!

Once beef has browned, add green pepper, and cabbage. Sauté for 3-5 minutes. Add tomatoes, tomato sauce, stock, oregano, basil, salt, and pepper.

Allow to come to a boil. Reduce heat, cover and cook for 45 minutes to 1 hour.

Contributed by Sugar Impact Diet Community Member Mary Cassler

Chicken Chili

MAKES 4 SERVINGS

INGREDIENTS:

- 1-2 tablespoons extra virgin olive oil
- 3 organic, free-range, boneless, skinless chicken breasts, cut into cubes
- 1 jalapeño pepper, minced
- 1 large onion, diced
- 3 garlic cloves, minced
- 2 teaspoons ground cumin
- 1 teaspoon ground coriander
- 1 teaspoon ancho chili powder
- 1 (4 oz.) can chopped green chilies
- 2 (14.5 oz.) cans cannellini beans, undrained
- 1 tablespoon dried oregano
- 1½ teaspoons sea salt
- ¼ cup fresh cilantro, chopped
- 2 avocados, sliced
- 1 lime

DIRECTIONS:

In a Dutch oven, heat olive oil over medium heat. Add chicken, jalapeño and onion and cook until lightly browned. Add garlic, cumin, coriander and chili powder. Cook for 1 minute longer.

Add broth, canned chilies, oregano and sea salt. Bring to a boil. Reduce heat to low. Rinse and drain 1 can of beans and add to the pot.

Leave the other can of beans undrained and mash with a fork in the can or with a potato masher. Add mashed beans with liquid to the pot. Cook for 20-30 minutes.

Taste for seasoning and adjust to desired heat level if necessary.

Serve with chopped cilantro and ½ sliced avocado per serving.

To get in your non-starchy vegetables, add some greens on top.

Contributed by Sugar Impact Diet Community Member Mary Cassler

Listen in to the
JJ Virgin Lifestyle Show podcast
for exciting guests, insider tips, and health
hacks you can use to take charge of your
own health. JJVirgin.com/podcast

Turkey and Vegetable Dal

MAKES 4 SERVINGS

INGREDIENTS:

- 4 tablespoons coconut oil, divided
- 1 teaspoon brown mustard seeds
- 1 teaspoon cumin seeds
- 10 fresh curry leaves, or 1 bay leaf
- 1 lb. lean ground turkey
- 8 oz. cremini mushrooms, sliced
- 1 medium onion, diced
- 1 jalapeño pepper, finely diced (remove seeds and rib for less heat)
- 2 tablespoons fresh ginger, grated
- 4 garlic cloves, finely chopped
- 3½ cups water
- 1¼ cup red lentils, rinsed
- 13.5 oz. unsweetened coconut milk
- 1½ teaspoon sea salt
- 1 teaspoon turmeric
- 1½ cups peeled butternut squash, cubed
- 1½ cups cauliflower florets
- 1 teaspoon garam masala
- 2 tablespoons fresh lime juice

DIRECTIONS:

In a large Dutch oven, heat 2 tablespoons coconut oil over medium-high heat. Add mustard seeds, cumin seeds, and curry leaves (if using) and cook until seeds begin to pop, about 20-30 seconds. Add mushrooms and cook until mushrooms brown, about 5 minutes.

Add remaining 2 tablespoons coconut oil to pan. Add turkey, onion, jalapeño, ginger and garlic. Cook, stirring occasionally, until turkey and onion begin to brown, about 5-6 minutes.

Add bay leaf (if using), water, lentils, coconut milk, salt and turmeric to the pot. Bring to a boil, stirring frequently to make sure the lentils don't stick to the bottom.

Add butternut squash and cauliflower. Return to a boil. Reduce heat to simmer and continue to cook, uncovered, stirring occasionally, about 20-25 minutes until the vegetables are tender and lentils are cooked through.

Turn off heat. Stir in garam masala and lime juice.

Contributed by Sugar Solution Community Member Mary Cassler

Thai Salmon with Coconut Quinoa

MAKES 4 SERVINGS

INGREDIENTS:

- 14.5 oz. unsweetened coconut milk
- 1 inch fresh ginger, grated
- 1 garlic clove, minced
- 1/8 red pepper flakes, use more if you like it spicy
- 1 tablespoon fish sauce
- ¼ cup fresh lime juice (juice from about 2 limes)
- 1 cup quinoa
- ¼ teaspoon sea salt
- 1/8 teaspoon freshly ground black pepper
- 4 6-ounce portions of wild salmon
- 1 red pepper, julienned
- 1 orange pepper, julienned
- 12 oz. yellow cherry or grape tomatoes, cut in half
- ¼ cup fresh cilantro, chopped
- ¼ cup pistachios, chopped

DIRECTIONS:

Preheat oven to 350°F.

In an 8 x 8 inch casserole or baking dish, mix coconut milk, ginger, garlic, red pepper flakes, fish sauce, and lime juice. Add quinoa and mix. Put in oven and bake for 10 minutes.

In the meantime, season salmon with salt and pepper.

After quinoa has been in the oven for 10 minutes, remove from oven and carefully place salmon on top of quinoa (salmon will poach in the coconut milk mixture) and top with peppers and tomatoes.

Place baking dish back into the oven and bake until fish flakes with a fork and the quinoa is fully cooked, about 30 minutes.

Serve each portion fish and vegetables with cilantro and 1 tablespoon of pistachios.

Contributed by Sugar Solution Community Member Mary Cassler

Breakfast Bites

MAKES 4 SERVINGS (MAKES 12 BITES, 3 PER SERVING)

INGREDIENTS:

- ¼ cup raw quinoa
- 3-4 cups non-starchy veggies of your choice (I used broccoli, scallions, peppers, and asparagus)
- ½ cup liquid (water, stock, or non-dairy milk)
- 4 slices bacon, chopped
- 8 pasture-raised eggs*
- coconut or olive oil to grease muffin pan
- Salt and pepper to taste
- Optional: thyme, paprika, nutritional yeast to taste

DIRECTIONS:

Preheat oven to 325°F.

Beat eggs and add all ingredients together.

Grease muffin pan. Fill muffin pan with egg mixture. Cook until eggs are done thoroughly (about 30 minutes depending on oven).

Note - if you use watery vegetables (such as tomatoes), do not add as much liquid to mixture.

* If not sensitive to eggs.

Contributed by Sugar Solution Community Member Nicole Lees

Skillet Ratatouille

MAKES 4 SERVINGS

INGREDIENTS:

- 1 tablespoon olive oil
- 1 red onion, chopped
- 1 tablespoon chopped garlic
- 1 small eggplant, chopped
- 1 medium zucchini, chopped
- 1 bell pepper, chopped
- 1 large tomato, chopped
- 1 tablespoon chopped fresh basil leaves, plus extra for garnish
- 2 teaspoons chopped fresh thyme leaves
- 2 teaspoons chopped fresh marjoram leaves
- 1 (15 oz.) can garbanzo beans
- ½ cup vegetable broth
- 1 tablespoon red wine vinegar
- Sea salt and pepper to taste

DIRECTIONS:

Heat olive oil in large skillet over medium heat. Add onion and garlic and cook, stirring occasionally until onions begin to soften, about 3-5 minutes.

Add eggplant, zucchini, bell pepper tomato, and herbs. Cook about 5 minutes.

Add garbanzo beans and vegetable broth and simmer 10-15 minutes until vegetables are tender.

Stir in vinegar and season to taste with salt and pepper. Garnish with basil leaves.

Sugar Impact Jambalaya

MAKES 6 SERVINGS

INGREDIENTS:

- 2 tablespoons coconut oil
- 1 large green pepper, diced
- 3 stalks of celery, diced
- 1 medium to large white onion, diced
- 2 cups okra
- 2 tablespoons garlic, minced
- ½ cup quinoa (can also use wild rice)
- 6 oz. chicken sausage
- 1 lb. chicken breast, cubed
- ½ lb. shrimp, peeled and deveined
- 1 (14 oz.) can crushed tomatoes
- 2 tablespoons Cajun seasoning (purchased, or make your own, below)
- 1½ cups stock or broth
- Salt and pepper to taste

MY CAJUN SEASONING:
- 2 teaspoons salt
- 2 teaspoons garlic powder
- 2½ teaspoons paprika
- 1 teaspoon black pepper
- 1 teaspoon onion powder
- 1 teaspoon cayenne pepper
- 1 teaspoon coriander
- ½ teaspoon dried oregano
- ½ teaspoon dried thyme

DIRECTIONS:

Heat pan to medium high. Brown sausage in casing and remove.

Add onions, peppers, celery and sauté until brown. Add okra, garlic, chicken and sauté until brown. Add seasoning and quinoa, sauté until brown. Add tomatoes and stock.

Add chicken sausage back in. Bring to a boil and then lower heat to a simmer. Cover and cook for about 40 minutes until quinoa, or rice, is al dente.

Add shrimp 10 minutes before serving.

Serve over spinach, or other greens, for added veggies and crunch. Top

Contributed by Sugar Impact Diet Community Member Nicole Lees

Chicken and Quinoa Bowl

MAKES 4 SERVINGS

INGREDIENTS:

- 1 tablespoon coconut oil
- 1 cup chopped red onion
- ¼ lb mushrooms, sliced
- 1 lb organic boneless, skinless chicken breast, thinly sliced
- ½ cup chopped carrot
- ½ cup chopped celery
- 2 teaspoons minced garlic
- 5 cups chicken or vegetable broth
- ¾ cup red quinoa
- 2 tablespoons fresh thyme leaves
- 2 tablespoons fresh parsley leaves
- 1/3 cup sliced kalamata olives
- Sea salt & pepper to taste

DIRECTIONS:

Melt coconut oil in large saucepan over medium heat. Add onion and mushrooms and cook stirring occasionally until lightly browned, about 5 minutes.

Add chicken, carrot, celery and garlic. Continue cooking an additional 3-5 minutes, stirring occasionally.

Add broth, quinoa, and herbs. Bring to a boil, reduce heat, cover and simmer about 15 minutes until chicken and quinoa are cooked.

Remove from heat, stir in olives and season to taste with salt and pepper.

Roasted Chicken and Lentil Soup

MAKES 4 SERVINGS

INGREDIENTS:

* 1 tablespoon olive oil
* 1 cup chopped yellow onion
* 1 cup diced red bell pepper
* 1 cup diced yellow bell pepper
* 1 tablespoon chopped garlic
* 1 small zucchini, halved and thinly sliced
* 1¼ cups green lentils
* 5 cups organic, low-sodium chicken broth
* 1 lb. cooked, roasted chicken breast, diced
* Sea salt and pepper to taste

DIRECTIONS:

Heat oil in large saucepan over medium heat. Add onion and bell peppers and cook, stirring occasionally, until softened, about 4-5 minutes.

Add garlic and zucchini. Continue cooking 1-2 minutes.

Add lentils and broth, bring to a gentle boil, reduce heat, cover and simmer about 35 minutes until lentils are tender.

Stir in the chicken and cook an additional 3-5 minutes until chicken is warmed through. Season to taste with salt and pepper.

NOTE: Before adding the chicken you can puree half the soup in a blender and return puree to pot then add chicken for a creamier texture.

Coconut Salmon Bites

MAKES 4 SERVINGS

INGREDIENTS:

- 2 baby bok choy, white and green parts separated
- 1 tablespoon coconut oil
- 2 shallots, chopped
- 1 jalapeño pepper, seeded and chopped
- 1 yellow bell pepper, chopped
- 2 teaspoons chopped garlic
- 2 teaspoons minced ginger
- 2 cups seafood or vegetable broth
- 1 (11 oz.) container unsweetened coconut milk
- 1 tablespoon curry powder
- 1 teaspoon ground cumin
- 1 lb. wild skinless salmon, cut into 1" pieces
- 1 (15 oz.) can cannellini beans, rinsed and drained
- Zest and juice of one lime
- Sea salt and pepper to taste
- 4 cups baby kale

DIRECTIONS:

Trim and thinly slice the white part of the bok choy and chop the greens. Set greens aside.

Melt coconut oil in large skillet over medium heat. Add white parts of bok choy, shallot and jalapeño pepper and sauté, stirring occasionally for 3-4 minutes until beginning to soften.

Add bell pepper, garlic and ginger and continue cooking 2-3 minutes.

Add broth, coconut milk and spices. Reduce heat and simmer 15 minutes.

Add salmon, bok choy greens and cannellini beans. Cook 5 minutes until salmon is opaque and greens are wilted.

Remove from heat, stir in zest and juice and season to taste with salt and pepper.

Serve over baby kale.

Find articles, recipes,
helpful online programs,
and more at
JJVirgin.com

ABOUT THE AUTHOR

Celebrity nutrition and fitness expert JJ Virgin (CNS, BCHN, EP-C) teaches clients how to lose weight and master their mindset so they can lead bigger, better lives. JJ is the author of four *NY Times* bestsellers: *The Virgin Diet, The Virgin Diet Cookbook, JJ Virgin's Sugar Impact Diet*, and *JJ Virgin's Sugar Impact Diet Cookbook*. Her latest book, *Miracle Mindset: A Mother, her Son and Life's Hardest Lessons*, explores the powerful lessons in strength and positivity that she learned after her son Grant was the victim of a brutal hit-and-run accident.

As co-star of TLC's *Freaky Eaters* and health expert on *Dr. Phil*, JJ is also a prominent TV and media personality, including regular appearances on *PBS, Dr. Oz, Rachael Ray, Access Hollywood*, and the *TODAY Show*. JJ also hosts the popular JJ *Virgin Lifestyle Show* podcast and writes for *Huffington Post, Rodale Wellness, Mind Body Green*, and other major blogs and magazines.

Find articles, recipes, helpful online programs, and more at www.JJVirgin.com.